Ready, Set, Write

Story Starters Grade 6

By
CINDY BARDEN

COPYRIGHT © 2003 Mark Twain Media, Inc.

ISBN 1-58037-241-4

Printing No. CD-1587

Mark Twain Media, Inc., Publishers
Distributed by Carson-Dellosa Publishing Company, Inc.

Table of Contents

Introduction to the Teacher

To some students, writing comes easily. To others, it's as difficult as brushing a crocodile's teeth!

Like most skills, writing takes practice. A person doesn't learn to play the harp, become a gymnast, or build a house without practice. By providing daily opportunities for students to improve their writing skills, you help them develop abilities they will use for the rest of their lives.

Learning to write well does more than help students take essay exams, write reports, and take notes. Writing helps students develop organizational, communication, and thinking skills.

Many of the topics and activities in this book are open-ended, designed not only to help students learn to write but to encourage them to write about topics of interest to them.

Students can use the activity pages for gathering ideas and prewriting. Prewriting includes jotting down ideas, arranging them in sequence, and writing a draft copy. They can write their final drafts on another sheet of paper.

Remind students to carefully proofread, revise, and self-edit their work before writing their final drafts. Peer edits and teacher edits also help students improve their writing. The Revising, Editing, and Proofreading Guide on page 2 can help students critique and improve their writing.

Other ways to improve student writing are to:

✿ Provide an audience for student writers.

✿ Prepare class or individual anthologies of short stories.

✿ Let students read their stories or essays to the class.

✿ Display student writing in the classroom, hallway, media center, and/or library.

✿ Encourage students to send editorials to school or local newspapers.

✿ Have students submit descriptive essays or short stories to the school newspaper.

✿ Let students work together to prepare a monthly class newspaper or create their own website featuring student work.

✿ Check the Internet and other sources for student writing contests, and encourage your students to participate.

Revising, Editing, and Proofreading Guide

Carefully reread what you wrote. Use the checklist below to revise and edit your writing.

Grammar, Spelling, and Punctuation

✔ Did you begin each sentence with a capital letter?

✔ Do all sentences have end punctuation?

✔ Do all sentences have subjects and predicates?

✔ Do your subjects and predicates agree with each other?

✔ Are all words spelled correctly?

✔ Did you capitalize all proper nouns?

✔ Do all of your sentences make sense?

Nonfiction writing

✔ Is your topic sentence interesting?

✔ Does your topic sentence express the main idea?

✔ Do all of your sentences stick to the main idea?

✔ Did you give specific examples?

✔ Did you present the main points in the right order?

✔ Did you leave out any important information?

✔ Did you include too much information?

✔ Does your conclusion sentence or paragraph sum up the main idea?

Fiction writing

✔ Are your characters believable?

✔ Is the dialogue realistic?

✔ Will the reader be able to visualize the setting?

✔ Is the character's problem or challenge clearly stated?

✔ Is the solution reasonable?

✔ Are the events arranged in a logical order?

Name: _____ Date: _____

Ideas, Ideas, Everywhere: *Writing Ideas*

Do you ever get stumped for writing ideas? Don't despair—ideas are everywhere. Many activities in this book will provide suggestions for essays and stories. Scattered throughout this book are other ideas in the "IDEA BANK" to save for another day.

When you think of a good writing idea, save it in your own idea bank. Jot it down before it floats off into the air and dissolves like a wispy cloud on a windy day. Save your ideas in a notebook or an old shoebox; any place will do as long as you can find them when you need them.

Personal Experiences: Unusual or amusing experiences can be good writing topics. Write some ideas on the lines below.

_____

_____

_____

Your bedroom is probably filled with writing ideas:
- Did you ever pretend that your old, battered stuffed animal was real when you were little?
- Do you remember who gave it to you and when?
- How about that old baseball mitt—the one you used to catch the pop fly for the third out in the last inning?
- Or was that the one you didn't catch?

Look around your bedroom. Write ideas for possible topics on the lines below.

_____

_____

_____

Memories are great writing topics. **Old photos** often bring back happy memories.
- Do you remember the day you got your first baseball cap?
- Or the day you went to the beach and found that seashell?
- How about the first time you spent the night at your grandparents' house?

Look through photos. Write ideas for possible topics on the lines below.

_____

_____

_____

Writing Tips

Whether you're sending an e-mail to a friend or preparing a ten-page report, following these tips will help you write better.

Decide on a topic before you begin writing.

- In an e-mail to a friend, the topic might be your vacation in Australia.

- In a report, the topic could be the effect of weather on classroom performance.

Narrow the focus of your topic.

- Your e-mail could focus on one particular event during your vacation, like a visit to a volcano or a ride in a glass-bottomed boat.

- Your report could focus on the effects of cloudy days on student performance.

Gather ideas.

- For an e-mail to a friend, gathering ideas may be a "think-about-it step."

- For a report, this would involve checking reference sources, doing surveys, gathering data, etc.

Organize your material.

- For your e-mail, you will probably tell what happened in sequential order.

- For a report, you could make an outline to organize the main ideas with examples or explanations for each main point.

Write the first draft.

- Don't worry if it gets messy as you cross out words or move sentences around.

Proofread.

- Correct errors in grammar, punctuation, and spelling.

Edit and revise.

- Make any other changes to improve your writing.

Rewrite.
- Write the final copy.

Double-check.

- Go back and read through what you wrote one more time.

Name: _____   Date: _____

A Mysterious Sound: *Topic Sentences*

A paragraph is a group of sentences about a specific topic. The **topic sentence** introduces the main idea of the paragraph. You should always write an interesting topic sentence to encourage the reader to continue reading.

Write three different topic sentences you might use to begin a paragraph about each subject below. Use your own paper if you need more room.

1. A mysterious sound heard at night: _____

    _____

    _____

    _____

    _____

2. Being lost: _____

    _____

    _____

    _____

    _____

3. An unusual dream: _____

    _____

    _____

    _____

    _____

4. A person you would like to meet: _____

    _____

    _____

    _____

    _____

5. Make an "X" in front of your best sentence for each topic.

6. Save this page to use with the next activity.

Name: _____   Date: _____

The Middle Provides Support: *Supporting Sentences*

Topic sentences are followed by **supporting sentences** that provide interesting information about the topic, give examples, or provide additional details and descriptions.

Write two sentences that could follow each topic sentence.

1. As the siren wailed, we grabbed our flashlights and raced for the cellar.

   _____

   _____

   _____

   _____

   _____

   _____

2. My memories of the best day of my life are as clear to me now as they were on that special, unforgettable day.

   _____

   _____

   _____

   _____

   _____

   _____

3. Rewrite your best topic sentence from the last activity. Add supporting sentences.

   _____

   _____

   _____

   _____

   _____

   _____

4. Save this page to use with the next activity.

Name: _____ Date: _____

Wrap It Up!: *Conclusion Sentences*

The **conclusion sentence** of a paragraph restates the main idea or sums up the main points in a paragraph.

Write two different conclusion sentences for each paragraph from the previous page.

1. _____

_____

_____

_____

_____

2. _____

_____

_____

_____

_____

3. _____

_____

_____

_____

_____

_____

4. Make an "X" in front of your best conclusion sentence for each topic.

5. Save this page to use with the next activity.

Name: _____ Date: _____

All Together Now: *Writing a Paragraph*

Writing Prompt: Write a paragraph using one of your topic sentences or conclusion sentences from the previous activities.

1. Topic sentence: _____

_____

_____

_____

2. Supporting sentences: _____

_____

_____

_____

_____

_____

_____

_____

3. Conclusion sentence: _____

_____

_____

_____

_____

_____

_____

4. Proofread, edit, and revise your work. Rewrite your final draft on your own paper.

** If you like any of your other ideas from these activities but you didn't use them, save them in your IDEA BANK.

Name: _____ Date: _____

Adults Need Recess Too: *Author's Purpose*

Authors write for many reasons:

A. to entertain
B. to provide information
C. to persuade
D. to express opinions

Determine the author's purpose for each example. Write A, B, C, or D.

1. _____ A newspaper article about a proposed new law

2. _____ A magazine article about an athlete

3. _____ A humorous article about eating spaghetti

4. _____ Directions for building a birdhouse

5. _____ An editorial about why people should not re-elect the mayor

6. _____ An article about why everyone should take a vacation in the Sahara Desert

7. Write a topic sentence for a humorous article about why adults should have recess.

_____

_____

8. Write a topic sentence for an informational essay about the benefits of riding a bicycle.

_____

_____

9. Write a topic sentence to persuade people to vote for you for mayor of your city.

_____

_____

10. Write a topic sentence that expresses your opinion about UFOs.

_____

_____

** Why adults need recess might be a good topic to save in your IDEA BANK.

9

Name: _____　Date: _____

Strange, But True: *Writing an Anecdote*

An **anecdote** is a short personal account of something unusual or amusing that actually happened. An anecdote might be about an unexpected surprise, an embarrassing moment, or a time when something turned out differently than you expected.

Writing Prompt: Write an anecdote about an unusual personal experience.

1. Topic sentence: _____

_____

_____

_____

2. Supporting sentences: _____

_____

_____

_____

_____

_____

_____

3. Conclusion sentence: _____

_____

_____

_____

_____

4. Proofread, edit, and revise your work. Rewrite your final draft on your own paper.

** Save ideas about other unusual situations or personal experiences in your IDEA BANK.

Name: _____   Date: _____

What If Ostriches Could Fly?: *"What If?" Ideas*

Asking **"what if?" questions** can provide many writing ideas. A question like "What if Snow White hadn't eaten the poisoned apple?" could provide ideas for writing different endings to that fairy tale.

"What if people could travel anywhere instantly?" could provide ideas for an exciting science fiction story.

For each topic, write a "what if?" question.

1. Television: What if _____
_____?

2. Cinderella: What if _____
_____?

3. Volcanoes: What if _____
_____?

4. Dinosaurs: What if_____
_____?

5. Parents: What if_____
_____?

6. Hands: What if _____
_____?

7. Wind: What if _____
_____?

8. The mayor of your city: What if _____
_____?

Writing Prompt: On your own paper, write the first draft of your narrative that answers one of your "what if?" questions. Include a title.

Proofread, edit, and revise your work before writing the final draft on your own paper.

**   Include "what if" questions in your IDEA BANK for future story ideas.

11

Name: _____ Date: _____

Tell Me a Story: *Organizing a Narrative*

A **narrative** tells about an event or series of events. The writer usually relates the events in the order in which they occurred (chronological order). Narratives can be fictional, like fairy tales, short stories, novels, or movies. Narratives can also be factual, like an account of what happened at school today, a news report on television, or an article in a newspaper.

Like other types of writing, a narrative should have a main point: a specific idea or event for the reader to focus on.

Follow the steps for writing a narrative about a holiday.

Step 1: List possible topics: _____

_____

_____

_____

_____

Step 2: Select one topic from your list: _____

_____

_____

Step 3: Narrow your focus. If your topic was birthdays, you could write a factual account of a particular birthday party or a fictional account of someone's birthday. List ideas that narrow the focus of your topic. Circle the one you like best. Mark it factual or fictional.

_____

_____

_____

_____

_____

_____

Continue your narrative writing on the next page.

Name: _____   Date: _____

Tell Me a Story: *Organizing a Narrative (cont.)*

Step 4: List words and phrases to describe events related to that specific topic.

_____

_____

_____

_____

_____

Reread your list of events. Cross out any that are not directly related to your specific topic.

Step 5: Put the events in order. Go back to your list of events and number them in order.

Step 6: Add details and specific information for each event.

One way to organize your narrative is to write one paragraph for each event you listed.

Write your narrative on your own paper. When you finish, proofread, edit, revise, and rewrite it. Share your narrative with a classmate or family member.

Name: _____ Date: _____

Getting to Know Your Characters: *Character Development*

Characters in stories can be people, animals, or objects. Characters can be realistic or completely imaginary. Characters can be based on someone you know or based on a combination of characteristics from several people. Knowing your characters well before you begin a story helps you write the story.

Create two people who could be characters in a story. Make one realistic and one completely imaginary. Fill in the two-page chart.

	Realistic	**Imaginary**
Name:		
Age:		
Occupation:		
When and where born:		
Physical description including hair, eyes, complexion, height, weight:		
Clothes usually worn:		
Best talent:		
Favorite hobby:		
Most important possession:		
Why is it important?		
Best quality:		

Name: _____ Date: _____

Getting to Know Your Characters: *Character Development* (cont.)

	Realistic	**Imaginary**
Worst bad habit:		
Describe best friend or pet:		
Type of people character likes:		
What annoys the character most?		
Best subject in school:		
Favorite place to be alone:		
Things the character likes:		
Things the character dislikes:		
Other details:		

Save your ideas about your characters to use with the next story-writing activities.

Name: _____   Date: _____

Flying Unicorns and Talking Gerbils: *Character Development*

Animals can be the main characters in a story. Like people, animals can be realistic or imaginary. A story about a dog who saves a child could portray the dog in a realistic manner.

Stories about imaginary animals could include real animals with human traits, like the three little pigs, the big bad wolf, the country mouse, and the city mouse. Animal characters can be completely imaginary, like a flying unicorn or a talking gerbil.

Fill in information about an imaginary animal that could be a character in a story.

Type of animal: _____

Name: _____

Physical description: _____

_____

_____

Special abilities: _____

_____

Describe where this animal lives: _____

_____

What does this animal like to eat? _____

What is unusual or special about this animal? _____

_____

What bad habit does this animal have? _____

_____

What good qualities does this animal have? _____

_____

What is this animal afraid of? _____

Why would this animal make a good character in a story? _____

_____

_____

Save your ideas about your animal character to use with the next story-writing activities.

**   If you have ideas about other animal characters, save them in your IDEA BANK.

Name: _____ Date: _____

A Sleepy Alarm Clock: *Character Development*

In the movie *Beauty and the Beast,* the characters were a combination of people, animals, and objects, like the animated teapot, clock, and candlesticks. Many authors have written stories featuring robots as main characters.

List other objects that have been characters in stories or movies.

Type of object(s)	Book or Movie
_____	_____
_____	_____
_____	_____
_____	_____

List five objects that could be characters in a story, giving a brief description of each one.

Example: a sleepy alarm clock that overslept and didn't ring when it was time to wake up someone

1. _____

   _____

   _____

2. _____

   _____

   _____

3. _____

   _____

   _____

4. _____

   _____

   _____

5. _____

   _____

   _____

Save these ideas about characters to use with the next story-writing activities.

** IDEA BANK: Page through magazines for pictures of people, animals, or objects you might use as characters in a story.

Name: _____   Date: _____

Pleasant Dreams: *Writing Dialogue*

When characters talk to each other in stories, it is called **dialogue**. The words they use and how they speak should match the type of character you want to portray. A conversation between two silly squirrels would be different than a discussion between a queen and a king.

Enclose the words a speaker says inside quotation marks. Begin a new paragraph each time a different character speaks. The example below shows the correct way to write dialogue.

"Why doesn't anyone trust me?" asked Little Alarm Clock as he rubbed the sleep out of his eyes.

"Maybe it's because you always oversleep," replied Grandfather Clock. "You simply are not dependable."

"I would be if I didn't have such great dreams," insisted the Little Alarm Clock.

Writing Prompt: Write dialogue that could take place between two of your imaginary object characters.

**   IDEA BANK: Listen to people talk while you ride on the bus or sit in a restaurant. Write down bits of interesting dialogue you might use in a story.

Name: _____ Date: _____

Molten Lava Bubbled and Hissed: *Setting*

The **setting** is where and when a story takes place and is an important part of a story. The setting can be in the present, past, or future. Stories can take place in real places or in ones that are completely imaginary.

Imagine a story setting for one of your people, animal, or object characters.

1. In what month and year will your story take place? _____

2. What is the weather like? _____
_____

3. Where does the story take place? Be specific. (For example: above the volcanoes of Jupiter; in a desert in Arizona; on a plane flying to Rome; in a dark cellar in Kansas).
_____
_____

4. Describe what your character would see when he or she looks around. _____
_____

5. What sounds does your character hear? _____
_____

6. What does your character smell? _____
_____

7. What can your character touch? _____
_____

   How does it feel? _____
_____

8. What might your character eat or drink? _____
_____

9. How does it taste? _____
_____

10. Other details: _____
_____

Save your ideas about a setting to use when you write your story.

Name: _____   Date: _____

The Troll Guards the Gate: *Plot Development*

The **plot** describes what happens in the story. It includes what the characters do, the problems or conflicts they face, the obstacles they overcome, and the consequences of their actions.

The plot could involve a character's personal problems. In the fairy tale, Cinderella did not get along with her stepmother and stepsisters.

1. Think of a story or movie that involves a character's personal problem. Write the title of the story or movie and the type of problem he or she has on the lines below.

    _____

    _____

The plot could be about a character's attempt to overcome physical obstacles, like sneaking past a huge troll guarding the gate to the castle or finding the way through a maze.

2. Write an idea for a physical obstacle your people characters might face in your story.

    Imaginary person character: _____

    _____

    Realistic person character: _____

    _____

The plot could involve a character's quest for a specific object (a buried treasure) or the answer to a question (who buried the treasure and why).

3. What object might your animal character be trying to find and why is finding the object important?

    _____

    _____

4. What question might your realistic person character be trying to answer and why is the answer important?

    _____

    _____

    _____

Save your ideas about plots to use with the next story-writing activities.

**   IDEA BANK: Even ordinary personal experiences can be changed and embellished to create the plot for fiction stories. Look what Dr. Seuss did in *And to Think That I Saw It On Mulberry Street!*

Sneaking Past the Troll: *First and Third Person*

In a **first-person story**, the only details that can be included are what that character thinks, sees, says, hears, learns, tastes, touches, and smells. Anyone else's experiences and thoughts cannot be included unless that character tells the main character about the events.

Example: As I watched the huge troll guarding the gate, I knew that getting past him was not going to be easy.

1. Write two first-person sentences about meeting a troll.

    _____

    _____

    _____

    _____

2. Write two first-person sentences about events inside a huge deserted castle.

    _____

    _____

    _____

    _____

A **third-person story** can include events and experiences of any character and even information that occurred before the story began.

Example: "Trolls might not be smart, but they are very strong. Maybe I can sneak past him," thought the knight.

3. Write two third-person sentences about the troll at the gate.

    _____

    _____

    _____

    _____

4. Write two third-person sentences about events inside the castle.

    _____

    _____

    _____

    _____

Name: _____ Date: _____

The End: *Conclusions*

The final part of a story is the **conclusion**: an explanation of how the character completed the quest, solved the problem, or found the answer. As a result, the character usually changes in some way, perhaps by becoming a stronger person or finding personal happiness.

Sometimes, the main character fails to complete the quest, or cannot solve the problem or find the answer. Then the conclusion may explain why that happened and how the character learns to live with the problem.

1. Select a personal problem and suggest one way your character could solve the problem or what he or she would do if the problem wasn't solved.

   _____
   _____
   _____
   _____
   _____
   _____

2. Select one of your ideas for a physical obstacle your character might face, and explain how the problem is solved.

   _____
   _____
   _____
   _____
   _____
   _____

3. Select one of the objects your character searched for, and explain whether or not it was found and what might happen as a result of finding or not finding it.

   _____
   _____
   _____
   _____
   _____
   _____

Save your ideas about solutions to use with the story-writing activity on the next page.

Name: _____ Date: _____

Putting It All Together: *Writing a Short Story*

Like other kinds of stories, a **short story** includes characters, setting, plot, and conclusion.

Writing Prompt: Use your ideas from the previous activities to write a story about one of your characters. Use your own paper if you need more room.

I. Characters
II. Setting
III. Plot
IV. Conclusion

_____

_____

_____

_____

_____

_____

_____

_____

_____

_____

_____

_____

_____

_____

_____

_____

_____

_____

_____

_____

_____

Proofread, edit, and revise your story. Write the final draft on your own paper. Title your story. Illustrations are optional.

Name: _____ Date: _____

Time for a Change: *Problem-Solving*

If you could make changes in your life, what would they be? Usually, when people want to make changes, it's because there are problems they'd like to solve.

1. What changes would you like to make at home?

_____

_____

_____

2. What changes would you like to make at school?

_____

_____

_____

3. What changes would you like to make in your community?

_____

_____

_____

4. What changes would you like to make anywhere else in the world?

_____

_____

_____

Read through your list of changes and think of possible solutions.

Writing Prompt: On your own paper, write about something you'd like to change. Explain why you think it should be changed, possible solutions, what might happen if this change is made, and what might happen if this change isn't made.

When you finish, proofread, edit, and revise your essay.

** Ideas about changes and possible solutions are good topics to save in your IDEA BANK.

Name: _____ Date: _____

Rugby and Pole-Vaulting: *Comparison/Contrast*

Many types of writing include examples of the ways in which two people, objects, or ideas are alike and the ways in which they are different.

Creating a Venn diagram can help you organize your ideas.

1. Write the names of two sports on the lines.

2. In the portion where the two circles overlap, list similarities. For example, both sports use balls.

3. In the portion of each circle that does not overlap, list things that are different. If you were writing about tennis and basketball, you might list "racket" on the tennis side and "team of five" on the basketball side.

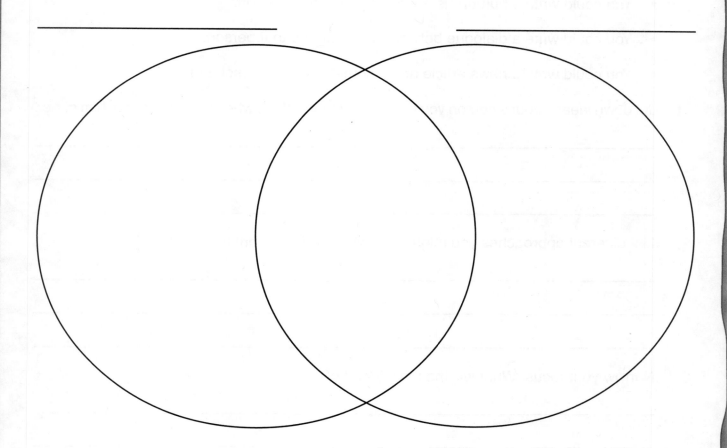

Writing Prompt: On your own paper, compare and contrast two sports. Include at least one paragraph explaining how the two sports are similar and one explaining how they are different.

Proofread, edit, and revise your work.

Name: _____ Date: _____

So Many Choices: *Different Approaches to Writing*

With most writing assignments, you usually have choices of how to approach the project. Here are some ideas you could use if your assignment is to write about a person you know.

- You could describe that person's character traits or focus on one particular trait, such as generosity or bravery.

- You could write a physical description of the person.

- You could write a poem about the person.

- You could make that person the main character in a play or short story.

- You could write about a particular memory you have of that person.

- You could write a humorous anecdote about that person.

- You could write a dialogue between yourself and that person.

- You could write a news article about something that person did.

1. Jot down ideas about a person you know and might include when you write about him or her.

    _____

    _____

    _____

2. List different approaches you might take when writing about that person.

    _____

    _____

    _____

3. Narrow your focus. What will the main idea be?

    _____

    _____

    _____

Writing Prompt: On your own paper, use your ideas to write about someone you know.

Name: _____   Date: _____

Twirled, Whirled, and Swirled: *Action Verbs*

Use lively **action verbs** like *hastened, twirled, bounced,* and *shuddered* to make your writing more interesting.

Lively verbs can change dull sentences into interesting ones.

Example: Dull: She was happy.

Interesting: She chuckled with glee.

Rewrite the sentences to make them more interesting by using action verbs.

1. She was afraid. _____

_____

2. I am sad. _____

_____

3. The cat was tired. _____

_____

4. They were lonely. _____

_____

5. The twins looked at each other. _____

_____

6. "I am leaving," he said. _____

_____

7. The whale swam away. _____

_____

8. The grass was green. _____

_____

9. The cheers were loud. _____

_____

10. She ate her pizza. _____

_____

Name: _____ Date: _____

Summer Olympic Games: *Writing an Action Paragraph*

Writing Prompt: Imagine being at the Summer Olympics. Write about the experience from the point of view of either a participant or a spectator. Use strong action words, and circle all the action verbs.

_____
_____
_____
_____
_____
_____
_____
_____
_____
_____
_____
_____
_____
_____
_____
_____
_____
_____
_____
_____
_____
_____

Proofread, edit, and revise your work. Rewrite your final draft on your own paper.

Hey, Diddle, Diddle: *Story Ideas*

   A nursery rhyme, poem, picture, news article, or even a cartoon could be a good start for a **short story idea**.

   To write a short story based on the nursery rhyme "Hey, Diddle, Diddle," you could start by asking questions.

Write answers to these questions about the poem.

1. What song did the cat play on the fiddle? _____

_____

2. Why did the cow jump over the moon? _____

_____

3. Why did the little dog laugh? _____

_____

4. When the dish ran away with the spoon, where did they go? _____

_____

5. Write two additional questions and answers about the nursery rhyme "Hey, Diddle, Diddle."

_____

_____

_____

_____

6. Write two questions and answers about any other poem or nursery rhyme.

  Title of poem or nursery rhyme: _____

_____

_____

_____

_____

Writing Prompt: On your own paper, write the first draft for a short story based on any nursery rhyme or poem.

Proofread, edit, and revise your story before writing the final draft. Be sure to add a title.

** IDEA BANK: Save ideas about other poems and nursery rhymes that could be developed into stories.

Name: _____   Date: _____

Brave, Heroic, Fearless, Gallant: *Synonyms*

Would you want to watch the same movie every day or reread the same book over and over? Most people would consider that very dull because they enjoy variety. When you write, synonyms provide variety for the reader.

Synonyms are words that have the same or nearly the same meaning. A thesaurus is a book of synonyms.

Write two or more synonyms for each word.

1. talk: _____

2. listen: _____

3. toddler: _____

4. asked: _____

5. glad: _____

6. loud: _____

7. afraid: _____

8. quick: _____

9. tame: _____

10. In the following paragraph, the word *cute* is used six times. Dull, dull, dull! Rewrite the paragraph. Replace the word *cute* with six different words.

Tyler was a cute baby. He wore cute shoes. He had a cute smile. His cute suit was blue with cute polka dots. Everyone thought he was so cute.

_____

_____

_____

_____

_____

_____

_____

Name: _____   Date: _____

What Would You Do?: *Writing a Paragraph*

Writing Prompt: Your favorite aunt came to visit for your birthday and brought you the ugliest sweater you have ever seen. You put it on to please her, but several of your friends are coming over, and you wouldn't be caught dead in public wearing the sweater. What would you do?

_____

_____

_____

_____

_____

_____

_____

_____

_____

Writing Prompt: Your parents asked you to watch your younger sister for an hour. About five minutes before they are due home, your friend stops by and asks you to go to a movie you really want to see. Your friend's older brother is driving, and they are leaving right now. What would you do?

_____

_____

_____

_____

_____

_____

_____

_____

_____

_____

_____

Name: _____   Date: _____

Fuzzy, Giggle, Moldy, Bitter, Squishy: *Sensory Words*

Sensory words describe the sights, sounds, smells, tastes, and feel of the world around you. Add five more words to the examples for each sense:

Sense	**Examples**	
1. Sight	square, fuzzy, wet	_____
	_____	_____
	_____	_____
2. Sounds	giggle, crunch, va-room	_____
	_____	_____
	_____	_____
3. Smells	chocolate, lemon, moldy	_____
	_____	_____
	_____	_____
4. Taste	sweet, creamy, bitter	_____
	_____	_____
	_____	_____
5. Touch	cold, soft, squishy	_____
	_____	_____
	_____	_____

Write sensory words to describe a barefoot walk through a field on a rainy spring day.

6. Sights: _____

_____

7. Sounds: _____

_____

8. Smells: _____

_____

9. Tastes: _____

_____

10. Touch: _____

_____

Name: _____ Date: _____

Clues to the Chocolate Cupcake Caper: *Writing a Sensory Paragraph*

Writing Prompt: Imagine being the first police officer at the scene of a robbery in a bakery. Someone stole all of the chocolate cupcakes! Use sensory words to describe what you see, hear, taste, smell, and feel as you investigate the crime and look for clues.

_____

_____

_____

_____

_____

_____

_____

_____

_____

_____

_____

_____

_____

_____

_____

_____

_____

_____

_____

Proofread, edit, and revise your work. Rewrite your final draft on your own paper.

** IDEA BANK: Pay attention to the sights, sounds, smells, tastes, and feel of items around you. Your senses provide opportunities for writing vivid descriptions.

Name: _____   Date: _____

Down in the Cellar: *Writing a Repetitive Poem*

Repetition can be used in stories or poetry for humor or to create a mood. Add one line to each stanza of the poem. The last word of the line should rhyme with grows and nose.

Down in the cellar where darkness grows,
Where the dust is so thick it clogs your nose,
You'll find a pair of old boots with holes in the toes.

Down in the cellar where darkness grows,
Where the dust is so thick it clogs your nose,

_____

Down in the cellar where darkness grows,
Where the dust is so thick it clogs your nose,

_____

Down in the cellar where darkness grows,
Where the dust is so thick it clogs your nose,

_____

Down in the cellar where darkness grows,
Where the dust is so thick it clogs your nose,

_____

Down in the cellar where darkness grows,
Where the dust is so thick it clogs your nose,

_____

Down in the cellar where darkness grows,
Where the dust is so thick it clogs your nose,

_____

Down in the cellar where darkness grows,
Where the dust is so thick it clogs your nose,

_____

Rhyming word suggestions:

arrows	blows	bows	clothes	compose	crows
elbows	enclose	expose	flows	foes	glows
goes	hoes	hose	Joe's	knows	lows
mows	oppose	pose	propose	prose	rose
shows	slows	sows	stows	those	tows

Name: _____   Date: _____

A Purple Cow With Round Spots: *Descriptive Adjectives*

Adjectives describe nouns. *Purple, round, sleepy,* and *shy* are adjectives. Adjectives help the reader form a clearer mental picture of a person, place, or thing.

For each noun, write several adjectives that would help the reader see exactly what you have in mind.

1. Child: _____

2. Bicycle: _____

3. Bear: _____

4. Jeans: _____

5. Cap: _____

6. Bed: _____

7. House: _____

8. Park: _____

9. Cup: _____

10. Shoes: _____

Complete the sentences by writing adjectives in the blanks.

11. The _____, _____ man with the _____, _____ hat hurried silently up the _____, _____ street.

12. As the _____ girl drew closer to the _____ trees, their _____ limbs seemed to reach out to grab her.

13. When the _____, _____ sun rose above the _____ rooftop, it looked like a _____ ball of fire.

14. Manuel found a _____, _____ bag in the _____, _____ alley behind the _____ theater.

15. The detective knew the _____ note and the _____ marks on the _____ door were _____ clues.

35

Name: _____   Date: _____

The Key–Be Specific: *Descriptive Writing*

Descriptive writing provides vivid details of how something looks, smells, feels, acts, tastes, sounds, etc. Description is a very important part of most types of writing.

The key to a good description is to be as specific as possible. The main purpose of a description is to help the reader visualize what you're describing, even if you're describing something you can't really see, like an emotion. Writers use many adjectives when writing descriptions.

1. Cut a picture from an old magazine that shows any type of scenery, preferably one without people. Do not show it to anyone.

2. Imagine being a part of the picture. List details you might see, hear, feel, taste, and touch if you were there in person.

_____

_____

_____

_____

_____

_____

_____

_____

_____

_____

3. Go back and add adjectives to make the details more specific.

4. Organize the details by numbering them in a logical way. Some ways to organize the details of a scene are to describe it from top to bottom or left to right.

Writing Prompt: Write a description of the scene on your own paper. Describe the scene so vividly that a reader would feel that he or she has been there.

5. Proofread, revise, and edit your description.

6. Write the final draft. Display your description with the picture of the scene for others to enjoy.

** When you come across an interesting picture, cut it out or make a copy and add it to your IDEA BANK.

Name: _____   Date: _____

The Big Bad Wolf Huffed and Puffed ... and Blew the House Down: *Cause and Effect*

CAUSE: The big bad wolf huffed and puffed.   **EFFECT:** He blew the house down.

For each **cause**, write a possible **effect**. Use complete sentences.

1. A winter blizzard covered the city in a blanket of snow nearly three feet deep.

    _____

    _____

2. Josh forgot to turn in his homework. _____

    _____

3. Sara studied hard before the big test. _____

    _____

4. The movie featured terrific special effects. _____

    _____

For each **effect**, write a possible **cause**. Use complete sentences.

5. They spent the day raking the lawn. _____

    _____

6. The winning athletes received gold medals. _____

    _____

7. By the time they arrived at the park, everyone was soaking wet. _____

    _____

8. The tearful baby finally fell asleep.

    _____

    _____

37

Name: _____   Date: _____

What's the Solution?: *Problem-Solving/Cause and Effect*

Writing Prompt: Write an essay to answer the question: What would make your neighborhood more pleasant?

1. Write a topic sentence describing one problem in your neighborhood. Be very specific.

   _____

   _____

   _____

   _____

2. Explain the cause(s) of the problem.

   _____

   _____

   _____

   _____

   _____

   _____

   _____

3. Describe the effect(s) of the problem. Use examples.

   _____

   _____

   _____

   _____

   _____

   _____

   _____

4. Propose a solution to the problem.

   _____

   _____

   _____

Proofread, edit, and revise your work. Rewrite your final draft on another sheet of paper.

38

Name: _____ Date: _____

What Happened?: *Finishing a Short Story*

Finish the following story.

Story Starter: With so many witnesses, it should have been easy for the police to discover exactly what had happened at the circus. However, no two people seemed to have seen exactly the same thing, even those sitting next to each other—like the twins, Carrie and Gary.

"It started when the clowns drove in on that motorcycle," said Carrie.

"No, it began with the elephants—definitely the elephants," said Gary.

_____

_____

_____

_____

_____

_____

_____

_____

_____

_____

_____

_____

_____

_____

_____

_____

Continue writing your first draft on your own paper. Proofread, edit, and revise your story, then rewrite your final draft. Be sure to add a title. Illustrations are optional.

Name: _____ Date: _____

How Do You ...?: *Writing Step-by-Step Instructions*

Answering the question "How do you ...?" involves providing instructions to perform a task. To be effective, your **instructions** should be very specific to provide all of the information your reader needs to accomplish the task.

Step 1: Begin by making a list of items needed to accomplish the task. This would include the tools needed as well as the ingredients or parts. Include all items, even the obvious ones. Be specific.

For example, if you were writing instructions for peeling an apple, you would need to specify the type of knife: butter knife, paring knife, steak knife, etc.

1. What items would you need to wrap a birthday present? _____

_____

_____

2. What materials and tools would you need to build a birdhouse? _____

_____

_____

Step 2: Make a list of instructions for the task.

3. Write a list of instructions for building a birdhouse or another task. If you choose to write instructions for another task, include a list of the materials and tools needed. Continue on your own paper. Give yourself extra room between steps, in case you need to add more information later.

_____

_____

_____

_____

_____

_____

_____

_____

Name: _____   Date: _____

How Do You ...?: *Writing Step-by-Step Instructions (cont.)*

Step 3: Check for missing information.

Check your list of steps for building a birdhouse or another task. Ask yourself if there is anything that needs to be done before the first step you numbered.

4. If yes, go back and add it now.

5. Read each step you wrote. Ask yourself if there is anything missing between one step and the next. Write in any transitional or missed steps.

By now, your list of steps is probably getting messy, but that's okay.

6. Continue filling in any minor steps you missed. Both the steps and the descriptions of how to do the steps should be as specific as possible.

Step 4: Number the steps in order.

A good way to organize your writing is to devote one paragraph to each major step in the process and include specific information and examples wherever possible.

Use transitional words, like *first, then, after that,* and so on.

7. Write the first draft of your instructions on your own paper.

8. When you finish your rough draft, trade papers with a partner. Work together to help each other fill in any missing information.

9. Proofread, edit, and revise your instructions. Then write the final draft.

**   For what other subjects could you write instructions? Save your "How To" ideas in your IDEA BANK.

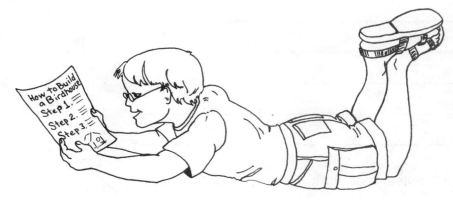

Name: _____   Date: _____

Polka Dots Everywhere!: *Writing Instructions*

> ### My Bread Recipe
>
> Put some stuff in a bowl, like flour, yeast, salt,
> and water. Mix it up, and then bake it in an oven.

What information is missing in this bread recipe? If important information is omitted in a recipe, the result could be a disaster! If steps or important details are omitted when writing instructions, readers can become confused.

Writing Prompt: Write specific instructions for painting a room blue with red polka dots. Include how to prepare the room, the equipment needed, and how to use the equipment.

_____

_____

_____

_____

_____

_____

_____

_____

_____

_____

_____

_____

_____

_____

Proofread, edit, and revise your work. Rewrite your final draft on your own paper.

Name: _____ Date: _____

Firsts: *Autobiographical Writing*

An **autobiography** is a true account that a person writes about his or her own life. It can include major events or focus on one specific event.

A great source of **autobiographical writing ideas** are some of the "firsts" in your life: the first time you walked to school alone, the first time you went to the dentist, the first time you rode a bike by yourself, etc.

1. List other "firsts" in your life that could be writing topics. _____

_____

_____

Writing Prompt: Write about a "first" in your life. Include a title.

_____

_____

_____

_____

_____

_____

_____

_____

_____

_____

_____

_____

_____

_____

_____

_____

2. Proofread, edit, and revise your work. Rewrite your final draft on your own paper.

**   Write notes about other "firsts" in your life in your IDEA BANK.

Name: _____   Date: _____

Combine These Elements: *Writing Fiction*

Select any four numbers between 1 and 10. You can use the same number more than once.

Write your numbers: _____; _____; _____; _____.

Match your numbers to the items in the corresponding columns of the four lists on the next page.

1. The first number = **main character**. Your main character will be:

    _____

2. The second number = **setting**. The setting for your story will be:

    _____

3. The third number = **time** the story takes place. Your story will take place:

    _____

4. The last number = **action**. The action for your story will include:

    _____

Writing Prompt: Use your imagination to write a short story that includes these four ideas. Combine them in any way you like.

_____

_____

_____

_____

_____

_____

_____

_____

_____

_____

_____

Write your first draft on your own paper. When you finish, proofread, edit, and write the final draft. Be sure to add a title. Illustrations are optional.

Name: _____   Date: _____

Combine These Elements: *Writing Fiction (cont.)*

Main Character (Your first number)

1. you
2. a dinosaur
3. a member of your family
4. a judge
5. a queen
6. a race car driver
7. a talking whale
8. a police officer
9. your teacher
10. a mystery writer

Setting (Your second number)

1. in the basement
2. at the Winter Olympics
3. on a soccer field
4. on a crowded bus
5. at the bottom of a deep, dark hole
6. in the school cafeteria
7. in the basement of an old building
8. at the post office
9. in a maze
10. in a hot, dry desert

Time (Your third number)

1. tomorrow
2. 1,000,000 years ago
3. in the summer
4. at noon
5. at dinner
6. during a blizzard
7. on a cold, damp night
8. on a Saturday in July
9. on Thanksgiving
10. during March

Action (Your fourth number)

1. investigating a crime
2. dancing alone
3. taming a wild animal
4. riding on a roller coaster
5. juggling
6. running for a political office
7. riding a bicycle
8. snowboarding
9. climbing down a steep mountain
10. taking bitter medicine

Name: _____ Date: _____

It Was a Dark and Stormy Night: *Cause and Effect*

Writing Prompt: Write about any weather event you've experienced. You could describe a severe or unusual weather event like a tornado, blizzard, or hurricane. You could also write about a scorching hot summer day; a severe spring thunderstorm; a blustery winter blizzard; a damp fall morning; or a day when the weather was absolutely perfect. Underline each cause. Circle each effect.

_____

_____

_____

_____

_____

_____

_____

_____

_____

_____

_____

_____

_____

_____

_____

_____

_____

_____

_____

_____

**   IDEA BANK: You don't have to be a meteorologist to write about the weather. Weather is something people can write about from personal experience.

Name: _____ Date: _____

Buy Kleenzbest Detergent: *Facts and Opinions*

Facts are statements that are true and can be proven. Facts are important when writing news articles, reports, and informational essays.

Opinions are statements that express someone's point of view. In advertisements, most types of essays, editorials, letters, and stories, writers include both facts and opinions.

Fact: Kleenzbest detergent has a lemony scent.

Opinion: Kleenzbest detergent smells better than real lemons.

You have just invented Kleenzbest detergent.

1. Write three facts about Kleenzbest detergent. _____

_____

_____

_____

_____

2. Write three opinions about Kleenzbest detergent. _____

_____

_____

_____

_____

3. Write a paragraph convincing shoppers to buy Kleenzbest detergent. Use both facts and opinions.

_____

_____

_____

_____

_____

_____

Name: _____ Date: _____

Shorter Vacations: *Writing an Editorial*

When people feel strongly about an issue, they write editorials to newspapers. An **editorial** expresses the writer's opinion about a topic. A well-written editorial clearly explains the issue, the writer's opinion of it, and specific examples or facts to help support that point of view.

Writing Prompt: What if the school board proposed making summer vacation only one month long and extending the school year to 11 months? How would you feel about this change? Write a letter to the local newspaper giving specific reasons for your opinion of this proposal.

Dear Editor:

_____

_____

_____

_____

_____

_____

_____

_____

_____

_____

_____

_____

_____

_____

_____

_____

_____

_____

**   IDEA BANK: Anything you have strong feelings about can be a good topic to write about. Save your ideas for future writing projects.

Name: _____   Date: _____

Brainstorming for Ideas: *Writing a Tall Tale*

Tall tales are stories about the adventures of characters with special or unusual abilities. Brainstorming is a great way to come up with writing ideas.

Get together with classmates, friends, or relatives. As you talk about story ideas, jot down any suggestions you like, even though you may not use them all. Often, one thought leads to more ideas. Before you know it, you'll have lots of fresh story ideas.

Brainstorm for ideas for a tall tale. Write down ideas for the main character, setting, plot, and conclusion on the lines below.

Character Ideas

Setting Suggestions

Plot Possibilities

Conclusion Thoughts

_____

_____

_____

_____

_____

_____

_____

_____

_____

_____

_____

_____

_____

_____

_____

_____

_____

Save your ideas to use with the activity on the next page.

Name: _____   Date: _____

Turning Your Ideas Into a Tall Tale: *Writing a Tall Tale*

After your brainstorming session, **organize your ideas** by selecting the ones you like most. Write words and phrases to clarify your ideas.

1. What does the hero or heroine of your tall tale look like?_____

_____

_____

_____

_____

2. What special abilities does that character have?_____

_____

_____

_____

_____

3. When and where will your tall tale take place?_____

_____

_____

4. Summarize the plot of your tall tale. _____

_____

_____

_____

_____

5. How will your tall tale end? _____

_____

_____

_____

6. Write your tall tale on your own paper. Proofread, edit, and revise your tall tale, and then rewrite your final draft. Be sure to add a title. Illustrations are optional.

Name: _____ Date: _____

Headlines Summarize: *News Articles*

    News articles provide information about an event. They are usually written in the third person. The headline of a news article summarizes the main point in a few words.

1. Cut out three articles from a current newspaper. Write the headlines below. Do not read the articles at this time.

    A. _____

       _____

    B. _____

       _____

    C. _____

2. Using only the headlines as a guide, write a sentence for each headline describing what you think will be the main idea of the article.

    A. _____

    B. _____

    C. _____

3. Read the articles. Did the headlines give good clues about the main idea of each article?

_____

    The first paragraph of a well-written news article should answer the questions *who?*, *what?*, *when?*, *where?*, *why?*, and *how?*.

1. Read the first paragraph of one of the news articles you cut out. Write the answers to the questions.

    Who? _____

    What? _____

    When? _____

    Where? _____

    Why? _____

    _____

    How? _____

    _____

Name: _____   Date: _____

You're the Reporter: *Writing a News Article*

Prepare to write a news article by answering the questions about an event you saw or attended.

1. Who (or what) was involved? _____

   _____

   _____

2. What happened? _____

   _____

   _____

3. When did it happen? _____

   _____

   _____

4. Where did it happen? _____

   _____

   _____

5. Why did it happen? _____

   _____

   _____

6. How did it happen? _____

   _____

   _____

7. What happened as a result? _____

   _____

   _____

8. Write a headline that summarizes the main idea of your article.

   _____

   _____

Writing Prompt: Use this information to write a news article about the event on your own paper. Include the headline in large print.

Name: _____   Date: _____

Today Is Your Lucky Day: *Finishing a Short Story*

Finish the following story.

Story Starters: You're babysitting for the neighbor's child. When he falls asleep, you decide to pick up his toys. As you reach for the toy telephone, it rings. Without thinking about how impossible that is, you answer it.

"Hello," says a voice. "Today is your lucky day."

_____

_____

_____

_____

_____

_____

_____

_____

_____

_____

_____

_____

_____

_____

_____

_____

Continue writing on your own paper. When you finish the first draft, proofread, edit, and revise your work before writing the final draft. Be sure to add a title.

Name: _____   Date: _____

Convince Me: *Persuading Your Audience*

To **persuade** means to convince someone to make a change, such as accepting a new idea, taking a specific action, or considering a different point of view.

To be effective, the author includes reasons why the action would be beneficial to the reader.

Writing Prompt: Write an article designed to convince readers to make a change. Include very specific reasons why the reader should make that change and how it would benefit the reader.

You can use one of these topic ideas or your own idea.

- Eat Right
- Donate Blood
- Wear Your Seatbelt
- Join a Health Club
- Recycling Is Important
- Take Your Next Vacation at the North Pole

_____

_____

_____

_____

_____

_____

_____

_____

_____

_____

_____

_____

_____

_____

**   IDEA BANK: Any subject you feel strongly about is a good writing topic.

Name: _____ Date: _____

And the Winner Is ...: *Writing an Example Essay*

If you could give someone you know an award, who would it be? What type of award would it be? You could give an award to your best friend, favorite teacher, or a person you most admire.

1. Fill in the blanks.

    This award for _____

    is presented to _____

    for _____

Writing Prompt: Write about the person who will receive your award. Give specific examples of why you selected that person.

_____
_____
_____
_____
_____
_____
_____
_____
_____
_____
_____
_____
_____
_____
_____
_____

After you proofread, edit, and revise your essay, rewrite it on fancy paper if possible. Give it to the person you wrote about as a special gift for a birthday, holiday, or perhaps for no occasion at all. It could be just to show the person he or she is appreciated.

Name: _____ Date: _____

Courage: *Defining by Example*

You can write about an abstract idea by defining an idea and giving examples.

Think about these questions:
- What does courage mean to you?
- Why is courage important?
- What makes a person courageous?
- What did you or someone else do that showed your, his, or her courage?

Writing Prompt: Write about courage and what it means to you. Include your definition of courage and an example of it.

_____
_____
_____
_____
_____
_____
_____
_____
_____
_____
_____
_____
_____
_____
_____
_____
_____
_____
_____

Proofread, edit, and revise your work. Rewrite your final draft on your own paper.

**   IDEA BANK: Other abstract ideas, like honesty, kindness, and friendship, can be good topics for essays or stories.

Name: _____ Date: _____

A Fun Place to Visit: *Writing a Review*

A **review** can describe items like software, artwork, movies, music, plays, books, and websites. A review can also describe places, such as museums, restaurants, or theme parks.

Before writing a review, the author watches the movie, eats at the restaurant, visits the theme park, and so forth.

A review includes what the author liked and disliked about the product, place, etc., and why the reader should or should not buy it, watch it, visit it, and so on.

Writing Prompt: Write a first-person review for a park or other recreational facility you have visited. Include reasons for what you liked and didn't like about it and your recommendation for the readers.

_____

_____

_____

_____

_____

_____

_____

_____

_____

_____

_____

_____

_____

_____

_____

_____

_____

_____

_____

Name: _____ Date: _____

Before and After: *Finishing a Short Story*

Read the sentence in the middle of the page. Write what happened before that event and what happened after it.

_____

_____

_____

_____

_____

_____

_____

_____

_____

Grandma turned the large brass handle on the heavy wooden door and slowly pushed it open.

_____

_____

_____

_____

_____

_____

_____

_____

_____

_____

Dear Cousin: *Writing an Autobiographical Letter*

An **autobiography** is a true account that a person writes about his or her own life. It can include major events or focus on one specific event.

You have received a letter from a cousin your age you have never met who lives in another country. Your cousin wants to know all about you: your school, your family, your home, your friends, your hobbies, etc.

Write a letter telling your cousin about yourself.

Dear Cousin,

_____

_____

_____

_____

_____

_____

_____

_____

_____

_____

_____

_____

_____

_____

_____

_____

_____

Yours truly,

_____

Name: _____ Date: _____

But What Happened First?: *Finishing a Short Story*

Writing Prompt: Read the ending of the story, and then write the beginning and the middle.

_____

_____

_____

_____

_____

_____

_____

_____

_____

_____

_____

_____

_____

_____

_____

_____

_____

_____

_____

_____

_____

_____

_____

They were so glad to finally be back on Earth that they never left again.

Name: _____ Date: _____

Dear Sir or Madam: *Writing a Business Letter*

People write **business letters** to request information, state opinions, express complaints, or send compliments.

Writing Prompt: Write a letter to a company requesting information about an item or service you might like to purchase. Address your letter to a specific person, if possible (Ms. Fussbudget, Professor Moriarty, etc.). If not, use a job title, like Manager, Director, etc.

In the letter, be very specific about what you want to know about the product.

Write your letter on your own paper. Use this format for a business letter.

Your name
Your street address
Your city, state, and zip code
Today's date

Name and/or title of person to whom you are writing, if known
Company name
Company street address
Company city, state, and zip code

Dear _____:

Yours truly,

Your name handwritten

Your name typed

50 Great Story Ideas

1. attending school in Sweden
2. becoming a king or queen
3. being a cartoon character
4. changing into a frog
5. dancing on a cloud
6. looking for buried treasure
7. finding buried treasure
8. exploring a comet
9. feeding dolphins
10. feeling wonderful
11. finding something you lost
12. frosting a cake
13. getting a pet camel
14. going over a waterfall
15. hearing an echo
16. joining the army
17. learning karate
18. living in a grass hut
19. losing your way in a cave
20. making a wish
21. marching in a parade
22. meeting a caveman
23. mixing a magic potion
24. moving to a new home
25. opening a door with no doorknob
26. overcoming a fear
27. packing for a vacation
28. receiving an Academy Award
29. riding in a helicopter
30. scoring the winning run
31. skateboarding
32. skipping school
33. sky diving
34. sleeping on a cloud
35. slipping on ice
36. stirring up a potion
37. sweeping feathers
38. swimming with dolphins
39. talking to a dragon
40. talking to a shadow
41. training a worm
42. traveling by camel
43. visiting Alcatraz Island
44. visiting Pluto
45. waking a grumpy elf
46. waking up after a bad dream
47. walking on stilts
48. wearing a suit of armor
49. weeding a garden
50. wrestling a tornado